You Might Be a ~~Crazy~~ Dedicated Hockey Mom If . . .

Jason Howell

illustrated by Braden Howell

Magenta Entertainment Ltd.

Library and Archives Canada Cataloguing in Publication Data

Howell, Jason, 1967-
    You Might Be a ~~Crazy~~ Dedicated Hockey Mom If . . .

ISBN 978-0-9687692-2-5

1. Hockey — Humour. 2. Mothers — Humour. 3. Mother and child — Humour. I. Title.

PS8565.0873Y682 2012   C813'.54   C2012-904830-5

Printed and bound in Canada

Magenta Entertainment Ltd.

THIS BOOK IS DEDICATED TO
ALL HOCKEY MOMS —
IT'S ABOUT TIME YOU RECEIVED
SOME ACKNOWLEDGEMENT . . .

AND TO SHANNON . . .
THE DRIVING IS ALMOST OVER.

— JH —

Introduction

Dear Hockey Mom,

Congratulations on having survived (so far) the "craziness" of your player's minor hockey career. Why is it crazy? Let's face it, if Mr. Freud himself were sitting in the stands these days — and took in all the over-competitive parents, the over-scheduled kids, and the 3-hour drives for the equivalent of 15 minutes of ice time — well, he would probably say everything had to do with whether or not your parents loved you and how strictly you were potty-trained; but, after that, I think he would say that all hockey parents are a little nuts. Some more than others . . .

I should clarify at this point, gentle reader — and honesty is important if we're going to have a "reading relationship" going forward — that I don't think you're "crazy" at all. Even if your heart sometimes takes you, unexpectedly, into battle to protect your player, I'm sure that everything you do is out of love and dedication (the "crazy" spectrum is quite broad, after all, so I'm betting you're on the "harmless" end of it). No, it's some of the other hockey parents who are outright crazy, and the fact that you have survived this long (without my book) is a testament to your courage and adaptability (and blind luck, let's be honest!).

This book (the one in your hand) will help you better identify (and avoid) the nuttiest hockey parents. You know the ones I'm talking about — they're not looking this way are they? In effect, what I'm offering you here is a full-blown rink survival guide. Need a reminder of the omnipresent dangers of arena life? Let's listen to a recent recording of a Caged-Lion Hockey Mom in action: "Hey ref, . . . can I talk to you for a minute? Ref, up here! That was clearly a slashing call against my kid! Even his father saw it (for once he wasn't out for a smoke break). He's no good, ref — that #7, I mean. If he hurts my boy, I'm coming for you . . . I'll need to find a sitter first, and I'll definitely need to clean the house before I go out, but make no mistake — I will eventually come for you!" A little scared? You should be! Make no mistake, then, THIS BOOK MIGHT JUST SAVE YOUR LIFE . . . At the very least, you can hide behind it when things get really ugly.

I hope you enjoy these hockey jokes and stories, as they're "all in good fun." I am not, of course, condoning the behavior of the over-the-top parent who berates their kid, their coach, the referee, or another parent. That's not cool. We all understand this, and yet all of us, even the best of us, have said and done things, "in the heat of the moment," that could register a little higher than we'd like on the "crazy meter." Sometimes, all we need is a humourous perspective to remind us where "the line" is, and (hopefully) this book offers just that.

Pre-Game (Psycho) Analysis

Most moms are nice. There, I got that out of the way. My mom is nice, and so is my mother-in-law. They come to the kids' games, and if there is a good play they simply strike both hands together, 2 or 3 times, rhythmically, while maintaining a prayer-like pose — "clapping," I guess you would call it. And sometimes they yell, "Way to go _____!" I cannot, to their eternal credit, remember a single time they were dragged away from the arena in handcuffs by the police. Maybe "acting up" just wasn't as popular in their day?

Anyway, not all hockey moms are as harmless as you, dear reader, and these two candidates for sainthood mentioned above. So, how do you figure out who on the team can't be trusted (with gossip) and who "has your back"? You might not have noticed this, but there are 5 basic hockey mom types, and these will be explored in the pages that follow. Your ability to recognize (and successfully avoid) the most dangerous types (the ones with the ESTROGEN PLUS PACKAGE) is the first step to surviving in the hockey rink habitat.

And now, WELCOME TO THE JUNGLE (please keep your arms inside the vehicle) . . .

A Field Guide to Hockey Mom Types

The Howler Monkey Hockey Mom
(Carayan Alouatta Andalona Mater)

Howler Monkey Hockey Mom

Game-day characteristics:
- *Loudest of the hockey moms.*
- *"Whoop-whoop-whooping" will have you scram-scram-scrambling for your earplugs.*
- *Provides non-stop, play-by-play of her kid's every movement.*
- *Often offers up loud "advice" for "opportunities" long since past.*

Range and habitat:
- *Likes to swing from the overhead heaters onto the top of the rink-side glass.*

Diet:
- *South Beach (with bananas).*

Life cycle and mating:
- *Will be fine until playoffs — then she'll have a "meltdown."*
- *Stares at opposing team's moms for long periods during a game — only to swing-attack them suddenly in a shrieking, showy scuffle.*
- *Uses a noisemaker, often a cowbell, to repel competing moms from her territory.*

The Bookworm Hockey Mom
(Anobii Undrstndsmi Mater)

Bookworm Hockey Mom

Game-day characteristics:
- *Slinks in unnoticed — and usually at the last minute — for games.*
- *Cross-over reading habits — reads more young-adult fiction when scared (in stands: often scared).*
- *Prone to making bizarre comments like: "All the kids played well" or "As long as they had fun."*

Range and habitat:
- *Reclusive and taciturn, this creature was only discovered in recent years, as she sits in high-altitude habitats: 12,000 feet up in the stands.*
- *Will occasionally migrate to lower elevations if she spots a like-minded bookworm mom below.*
- *Often has no interest in hockey, and "never really wanted to move to this barbaric, backwater town in the first place."*

Diet:
- *Sophie Kinsella; Kristin Hannah — anything without violence (or sports).*

Life cycle and mating:
- *Not much is known — lives a life under covers.*

The Caged-Lion Hockey Mom
(Asinuss Dwellonum Mater)

Caged-Lion Hockey Mom

Game-day characteristics:
- *Follows the play wherever it goes, pacing back-and-forth along the boards.*
- *If her player is on a breakaway, she is inclined to run the entire distance of the arena beside him — as though she herself were "home free."*
- *Pounds the glass repeatedly (as though trying valiantly to escape her lot in life).*
- *Obsessed with the referee: complains about his "poor eyesight" and his blatant attempts to blacken the name of her family, especially of her kid, who "has excellent manners and obviously never deserved a penalty on that play."*

Range and habitat:
- *Roams the arena for prey before and after games.*
- *Has been known to promise referees "a visit when they least expect it."*

Diet:
- *Has been known to attack (and swallow whole) bookworm hockey moms.*

Life cycle and mating:
- *She wears the pants in the family — husband cleans and irons them.*

The Mama Bear Hockey Mom
(Ursus Major Penaltum Mater)

Mama Bear Hockey Mom

Game-day characteristics:

- *Does not get distracted (or angered) by the sight of vertical stripes.*
- *Sometimes knits toques or scarves in the stands.*
- *Seems like the most calm and rational mom you've ever met . . . until there is a perceived on-ice threat to the safety of her kid. Then, run; don't stop; don't look back; just run for cover . . .*

Range and habitat:

- *Most likely hockey mom to be Bringer of the Group Blanket, and to sit thereon.*
- *Never moves during games, and follows the play closely (even when you think she's not paying attention).*

Diet:

- *Tea and biscuits (and sometimes nuts and berries from the vending machines).*

Life cycle and mating:

- *She keeps the hockey family together, and can often be seen grazing at the concession stand with her younger cubs.*

The Poison Dart Frog Hockey Mom
(Terribilis Emailum Mater)

Poison Dart Frog Hockey Mom

Game-day characteristics:
- *Proudly sports the bright colours of her team.*
- *Sometimes so cleverly camouflaged that no one notices when she actually ends up on the ice.*
- *Claps at all the right times.*
- *Highly toxic communication through iphone or Blackberry.*

Range and habitat:
- *Will follow the movements of, and interaction between, only 2 people: her player and the coach.*

Diet:
- *Lives on small insects and beetles, and has excellent vision for seeing things that no one else does.*

Life cycle and mating:
- *No longer waits for predators to attack her player — proactively sends nasty emails to the coach and parents after games.*
- *Mate usually stands at the opposite end of the rink (and stays offline).*

You Might Be a Crazy Dedicated Hockey Mom If . . .

- *Your hairdresser asks if you want to "keep the hockey hair look."*

- *You find yourself stressed out and crying in the car on the way to a game, not because of the blinding snowstorm and 0% visibility, but because you're running late.*

- *After all these years . . . you still can't understand why anyone is hitting your kid in a contact sport.*

You've taken the time to add up what you're actually
spending each month on hockey —
and you still keep going . . .

You Might Be a ~~Crazy~~ Dedicated Hockey Mom If . . .

- *You're willing to pass up a beautiful summer day at the beach for an extra power skating session (freezing-to-death) at the rink.*

- *You've started to rank hotels based solely on 2 criteria: 1) Do they have a pool? and 2) Do they allow mini-stick play in the hallways?*

- *You now consider sweat pants at the rink a "good look."*

In your house, there's no such thing as a calendar —
there's only a "hockey schedule."

You Might Be a Crazy Dedicated Hockey Mom If . . .

- *You seem to have a thorough understanding of <u>BOTH</u> the offside and icing rules.*

- *You've told the coach that it would be MORE FAIR if your player were on the ice EVERY SHIFT.*

- *You've spent a lot of time teaching your player patience, not because it's a virtue, but because you know that revenge is a dish best served cold (and you have a great memory for jersey numbers!).*

You've happily accepted the newly created (and self-appointed) role of "TRAINER OF MY OWN KID."

You Might Be a ~~Crazy~~ Dedicated Hockey Mom If . . .

- *You think the gap-toothed look is a turn-on.*

- *You would definitely consider sleeping with the coach (equipment manager, trainer, . . . or rink maintenance guy) if it meant more ice time for your kid.*

- *You chose your last family vehicle not based on mileage, or even any kind of safety rating — easy choice really: it was the only one that could fit all the hockey bags.*

You've asked, albeit politely, for one of the weaker players on the team to be traded.

You Might Be a ~~Crazy~~ Dedicated Hockey Mom If . . .

- *You see all this slashing, hitting, and fighting as an excellent way for your player to make friends.*

- *You drank only Gatorade when you were breastfeeding.*

- *You've given proper organization to the dissemination of gossip this year, insisting that it be communicated in ascending order by jersey number.*

You're planning to play a more active role in all the "hockey politics" this year.

You Might Be a ~~Crazy~~ Dedicated Hockey Mom If . . .

- *The love you offer your children is definitely unconditional — as long as they try their hardest on the ice.*

- *You've taken it upon yourself to sew a "C" on your player's jersey, even though the team already has a captain.*

- *You're always quick to let people know where they stand with you, and usually where they end up standing is at the other end of the rink.*

The "hockey vehicle" stinks to high heaven,
but you just don't care any more.

You Might Be a Crazy Dedicated Hockey Mom If . . .

- *The last time your husband bought you jewelry it came from a table vendor at a hockey tournament (and you're okay with that).*

- *You've started to prefer re-runs of the Original Six to (distant) memories of Original Sex.*

- *You have a hockey tattoo that (almost) no one knows about.*

You've tried to strangle someone (recently)
with your spirit scarf.

You Might Be a ~~Crazy~~ Dedicated Hockey Mom If . . .

- *You can magically produce extra underwear and socks at will.*

- *You've complained to the school principal that the kids should be allowed to play more road hockey at recess.*

- *You'll drive the kids wherever they need to go for hockey, at a moment's notice, without complaint — now that's crazy!*

Your arm automatically goes up
when a penalty should be called.

You Might Be a ~~Crazy~~ Dedicated Hockey Mom If . . .

- *Your husband's job at team gatherings is mainly to circulate, . . . to circulate and apologize for your behaviour earlier.*

- *You've bought a referee uniform for "role-playing night."*

- *You believe there are only 2 things worth shouting in this life: "Skate!" (when your player has the puck) and "Pass the Puck!" (when he doesn't).*

You usually bring enough wine to hockey tournaments
to feed (or water?) an entire army.

You Might Be a ~~Crazy~~ Dedicated Hockey Mom If . . .

- *You've forgotten what the kids look like with their helmets off.*

- *People have compared your role as hockey mom with Christian Bale's performance in Dark Knight.*

- *You've had your C-section scar enlarged, so you'll look tougher.*

Your team wants the fans to be their "6th man" —
and sometimes you literally are.

You Might Be a ~~Crazy~~ Dedicated Hockey Mom If . . .

- *You've found yourself gossiping about a kid to that same kid's parents.*

- *You had to quit your job and become a stay-at-home mom, just to keep up with all the hockey.*

- *It's not unusual for people at the rink to stop mid-conversation to ask you, "and who (or which personality) am I speaking with right now?"*

*You and the coach don't exactly see eye-to-eye on the
"importance of manners and showing some class."*

1st Period Intermission

THE BEST OF JENNY G'S

HOCKEY MOM BLOGS*

*includes blog entries that Jenny couldn't figure out how to upload to her website.

Ladies, this is a picture of Yours Truly, Jenny G, lounging with my new friend, Margarita, after a big end-of-year tournament — remember to celebrate!

Jenny G's Hockey Mom Blog #1

Hockey Blanket Etiquette for Dummies (and for Smart People, Too!).

OK, hockey moms, I really must share this story with you. At last night's Major Atom game in Oakville, something truly outrageous happened. She-Who-Must-Not-Be-Named tried (unsuccessfully) to sit on Marge's hockey blanket. As everyone (who's anyone) reads this blog is 100% aware, only Marge, Patty and I — the Three Hockey Momketeers — have sitting rights sewn up on that bum-warming blankie.

Yet here she was, Lady-No-Name, just waltzing on over to us before the game, with not a care in the world (between you and me, I'd have a care or two if I were her, after what she pulled at last month's tournament . . . though, as we all know, "what happens at a tournament, stays at a tournament"). Anyway, back to the story, she fakes left, then right . . . next thing we know, she's practically sitting in Patty's lap.

THERE WAS NO ROOM ON THE BLANKET, PEOPLE!

Besides, I thought everyone knew — isn't it obvious? — that blanket-sitting is by invitation only . . .

We had to ask her to leave the blanket immediately, which she did (abruptly, with a little helpful push from Patty). The bruises suffered as she bumped-bumped-bumped down the bleachers were, as Marge later explained to her, "part of the territory when you play a contact sport."

I am appealing to hockey moms everywhere: please show respect for the blanket. If the Bringers of the Blanket want you to share it, you'll receive an invitation (formal, by email). While on the blanket, you will observe and mimic the mannerisms of the Blanket-Bearer: cheering when she cheers; laughing when she laughs; and waving your arms wildly and in tandem when the ref makes "another bad call." You can't just go to the park and plant yourself down on someone's picnic blanket, can you? Emily Post herself would not allow your wayward buns to just come along uninvited and plunk themselves down on her hockey blanket.

Patty has asked — demanded, really (she scares me!) — that I remind everyone to stay off Marge's blanket unless you receive a "formal invitation in those Palmolive-soft hands of yours." This is not really my style — but I've worked too hard to get on this blanket to blow it now . . .

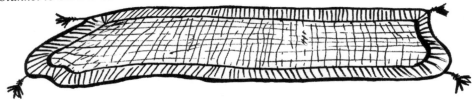

Jenny G's Hockey Mom Blog #2

I Am a Hockey Fashionista

There's no reason, dear reader, why you can't look more stylish at the rink, while, at the same time, choosing a winter wardrobe that hides those inevitable (yes, they are inevitable) extra one or two hockey season bulges. Yes, you, too, can be a Hockey Fashionista if you follow these tips:

Shoes

High heels are just plain dangerous. One of my girlfriends went straight from the game to the hospital last week, after she got her heel caught in a dressing room floor drain. It's true, they raise and accentuate your buttocks, but you can achieve the same effect by simply wearing tighter Calvin Klein's. In a nutshell, your shoes should reflect your personality (but — hint, hint — the world has enough "sensible" shoes . . .).

Pants

If you simply must wear sweat pants, at least wear designer sunglasses as well: that way you'll look like someone fun; someone who partied hard last night, rather than someone who wild horses couldn't pull away from the Party Mix bowl.

Sweater

A soft cashmere speaks volumes: it says, "I'm not crazy like some of these other hockey moms. Look here — see how soft I am?" And so what if you've gained a roll or two in the winter — at least you'll look warm and cuddly. The team sweater, on the other hand, is the fashion equivalent of wearing a giant hazard warning sign.

Spirit Scarf

A spirit scarf in team colours is both fun and practical, showing your support of the team and keeping you warm at the same time. On the downside, however, it can give enemy moms a choke-hold advantage in post-game scuffles (thanks to Patty for reminding us of this last Friday!).

The Toque (and HAIR)

The toque, and I shouldn't even need to mention that it MUST MATCH THE SCARF, is where you can run into some serious "rink-hair trouble." My suggestion is to keep your toque on, and curl your hair up over the bottom; it'll look sassy and sporty, like you just came in from a rousing snowmobile ride. Leave nothing to chance, though — spray everything!

Jenny G's Hockey Blog #3

Ice Time Is a Precious Gift

We are on this earth, ebbing and flowing with its tides, for too short a time, my friends; we should enjoy every second that our child is playing hockey, carefree and happy. Unfortunately, back to reality, sometimes they're only on the ice for a few seconds — victims of the coach-turned-God, who seems to think our kids are best-suited to "warm the bench."

For years, I just watched the games, wondering if Alex got a fair shift that night; it was hard for me to tell, honestly, because I never kept track of the time. When Alex wasn't on the ice, I would just stare at him on the bench (trying to guess what he was thinking).

It was his 2nd year of hockey when I had an epiphany: I saw that all the other parents had stopwatches. They kept them slightly hidden: one would hide behind a garbage can to look at it; another would have his arm around his wife, and check it secretly behind her back. For years I thought Tanner's dad had a drinking problem, because his head would occasionally disappear inside his jacket (like some kind of turtle-man), only to pop out fuming red. Little did I know that he was suffering from hockey enlightenment: checking his stopwatch to confirm his worst fears — Bobby had been short-shifted "ONCE AGAIN."

Here's the secret, ladies: I don't know anything about hockey; I don't even know how a stopwatch works; but I do know, now, thanks these other parents, how to protect my kid's ice time. All I do is hold up my stopwatch during games — why hide it? — and then, at random moments, I jump to my feet and yell stuff like, "Bloody hell, 30 seconds!" or "He barely got out there." "But," you ask, "what if I don't yell these things at the right time?" You worry too much. If it's at the wrong time, the coach will think you're referring to an earlier play (besides, he's too busy watching his own kid anyway). Do it my way, and I guarantee your player will start getting longer shifts.

I know Marge keeps a "mileage log" of how much time her Tommy plays each game. That seems like a lot of work to me, and I'd never be able to remember to email the coaches after every game like she does — she's a saint!

Remember, hockey moms, ice time is a precious gift — one worth protecting.

Jenny G's Blog #4

The Fundraising Committee Came to Call

Well, it's the time of the year that everyone loves (to hate): fundraising time! With Alex's new Minor Peewee team — I'm not sure if other hockey moms can relate to this or not — the fundraising committee is run much like a secret society: no one knows who belongs to the committee and is making the decisions; as parents, all we know is our "mission" on any given day, usually at the last minute (and often to no apparent profit).

The other day, for example, I was assigned the task of handing out vegetables to people as they left the rink. I'm not sure how having me do that helped raise money for more power skating?

Then, yesterday, someone slipped a note under my door at home, telling me to break another team's manager's hand. Apparently that team had a dance booked on the same day as ours, and some genius on our fundraising committee thought breaking their manager's hand would make them pull out of that time slot. I guess lower ticket prices never occurred to him? And who do they think I am — Tonya Harding? Although, to be 100% honest, which Coach says is an important quality if I want to be with "The Group," I'm tracking that manager's movements as I write this, because if I don't break his hand they'll take it out on my Alex (and play him less).

The Fundraising Committee — or the "Brotherhood" as they call themselves in email communications — has decided that the blank cheques we gave them at the start of the year were "less than satisfactory." They have instituted a 10% "Power Skating Tithe," to be withdrawn from our personal bank accounts on a weekly basis (I'm going to take a stand — and push them for bi-weekly).

We have also been told that "any and all vacation requests must be submitted 3 years in advance," and that "any parents silly enough to request vacation time during playoffs will be subject to 1000 family push-ups."

I have to run . . . I've said too much . . . someone's following me . . . "Hi, Guys . . . like I told you before, I'm totally okay with the Power Skating Tithe . . ."

Someone feed my family if I don't make it . . .

Jenny G's Blog #5

What Does Teamwork Really Mean?

Happy Valentine's Day, hockey moms! Hope you got something that tickled your fancy (or at least some part of you!). I made cupcakes for our Major Peewee team earlier today, and, as I was waiting outside their dressing room door to deliver them, I just happened to catch the last part of Coach Hegoesonandon's post-game talk. This is a bit embarrassing, but when I heard Coach talk about the importance of teamwork, I burst out crying like a baby. If Alex wasn't embarrassed of me before . . .

Coach Hegoesonandon opened the door, and he just stared at me, all befuddled — the same way my Bob (or any man) looks when confronted with a woman's emotion.

"What's this?" he asked. "Some heart? That's just what these kids need. Come in and talk to them, Jenny. Share with them not just your cupcakes, but your thoughts on teamwork and heart."

That was his first mistake. I'd had a long day, and my Valentine's Day present was a less-than-romantic weed whacker.

I went into that locker room, and standing in its centre, found myself looking into 16 sets of red and tired eyes.

"Boys," I began, "You may have lost this game, but you played with more teamwork on that ice today than most of your dads have ever showed around the house. You, young Jack Jr., when was the last time your dad vacuumed the carpets? And Mickey, is your dad not capable of folding his own underwear? Boys, is it really so hard for men to work together with their wives? Listening to them, and treating them as equal teammates? I'm getting so tired of doing everything myself . . ."

And with that, I left the room. Coach Hegoesonandon is probably still shaking his head.

INSTANT UPDATE: I just got an email from Coach: apparently, we now have a "no-parents-in-the-dressing-room policy." Go figure!

By the way, here's a picture of my cupcakes:

Jenny G's Blog #6

Who Controls the Overhead Heaters?

Any veteran hockey mom worth her weight in goalie gear will tell you that the key to rink survival is your ability to quickly locate the overhead heaters in out-of-town arenas. Look up, people! If you can't find that heater within 47 seconds of entering the arena, it's goodbye Whatever-Your-Name-Is and hello "Frozen Lucy."

Feedback from my blog readers has led me to the conclusion that the overhead heaters are also a good conversation piece: people ask (careful to hide the tone of desperation), "Are those things turned on yet?" and "Any heat being thrown your way?"

Curiously, though, we treat the question of if and when the heaters will be turned on as though it's one of nature's mysteries. Take a moment to let this sink in, dear reader, as IT'S A MATTER OF LIFE AND DEATH: someone is controlling, with a flip of a switch, whether or not the heaters come on. Who controls this? Some would say God; others, the maintenance guy. In either case, I don't want to see any more hockey moms freeze to death beneath inactive heaters.

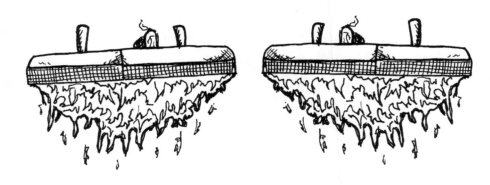

What should you do if the heaters are off? You can either pray for them to be turned on (which sometimes works), or you can go for a little walk to the rink maintenance office and knock-knock-knock your way to Toasty Buns Land.

What you can never do — even if you're cold and desperate — is try to sit on a rival hockey mom's blanket. You do this and you'll be warm alright — you'll be so warm, you'll be TOAST!

Is it too early for another secret? The rink staff are also Keepers of the Washroom Key, and, rumour has it, they are the Openers of that Large Rectangular Box that Hides the Coffee.

Remember to keep your head up (and stay warm), hockey mom!

Jenny G's Blog #7

How a Rep Team is Picked

I get so nervous when try-outs are just around the corner (as they are now, for Alex's Major Bantam year), and I thought it might help calm my nerves a bit to talk about how the whole process works . . . Let me just get my red wine — I'll be right back.

OK, so here's the scoop: the Executive Committee, a group bound together by no small degree of self-interest and a long memory of each other's previous errors and personal failings, agree to put all that behind them in the pursuit of a like-minded coach for your team. Who is this coach, you ask? The applicant is, from my experience, usually someone who is:

> *a) Unhappy with how his own playing career ended*
> *b) Consumed by extreme anger to wake up every day and find himself still alive*
> *c) The father of the weakest player on the team*
> *d) The worst communicator on the planet*
> *e) Free most evenings and weekends*

The Executive then interviews the applicants, and picks the one who best fits most of these criteria.

The new coach, upon hearing the happy news, drives directly to the nearest pub to meet the parents pre-selected to fill out his bench staff positions. They have been carefully chosen, based on there being a "snowball's chance in hell" that their kids will outshine his own. He then proceeds to offer them the roles least suited to their natural abilities: the spendthrift is named manager; the most aggressive person becomes trainer; and the person least inclined to follow orders, the role of assistant coach. Having now put in place the ingredients for a "long season," their best decision (and only hope) is if, in desperation, they have the common sense to turn to one of the wives for help — at least we know how to organize and multi-task!

By the time try-outs roll around, half of the team has already been picked and their parents are on the bench (or "helping out" in some way). And then, after try-outs, the parents on the team will have to choose 1 of 3 "camps," sort of like Survivor:

1) The coach's corner (with the coach and, sometimes, his wife)
2) The forever disgruntled
3) The completely disinterested

Together, you'll spend an entire year trying not to kill each other, but you'll always have one thing in common — the art of second-guessing the coach.

Jenny G's Final Blog

My Hockey Gratitude

Well, hockey moms, the season is winding down, and I think we can all agree (except maybe Susan) that it's not a moment too soon. The early mornings practices, the long drives to games, and the image of Susan sleeping with my Bob are all things that we will hopefully look back on with, at the very least, a little less rage in the future.

I will always remember our goalie, Omar . . . I think you could drive a bus through that 5-hole at the start of the year, and at the end . . . well, at least it didn't seem like all the bus traffic was actually being directed through there. By the way, I think we could all learn a thing or two from the website ismychildbowlegged.com . . .

And let's not forget Coach Vinnie. I would like to take this blog moment to thank him personally for allowing us that one hockey-free weekend (Christmas), and for the new words of the 4-letter variety that he taught our children whenever the score was not in our favour.

And OMG, what a great philosophy he had about booking us in the best hotels for tournaments, and then refusing to let the kids go swimming. We can only hope and pray that this mental giant gets the team again next year.

"Trainer Rick also deserves some thanks," you say. Of course, how could we forget his slipping and sliding to the rescue of every injured player (we really should have dipped into the team funds to buy him no-slip shoes . . . Brian estimates that Rick fell on about half of the kids he worked on — a shout out to Bobby P., who's still in traction, by the way). The trainer's course (curse?) might be the highest level of education Rick ever receives . . . and we should all be thankful he took "the path more taken," and decided not to go into the medical profession.

And cheers to the door-openers, Squeeky and Little Mike! You definitely, . . . well, you definitely opened the doors this season. You seemed to pay more attention to what was happening on the ice as well, and thanks for being sober around the kids (most of the time).

Finally, a big thanks to Susan, for finding the time in what was a very hectic hockey schedule to sleep with my Bob an estimated 14 times — now that's extra effort!

You Might Be a Crazy Dedicated Hockey Mom If . . .

- *You refuse to shave your legs during playoffs.*

- *You don't need to rush after opposing fans to catch them . . . everyone who knows you has complete confidence that, as you move slowly towards them, you will eventually catch them.*

- *You get upset if the clothes washer doesn't have enough puck dents on it.*

You rank playing house league hockey right up there
with getting struck down by leprosy.

You Might Be a Crazy Dedicated Hockey Mom If . . .

- *Let's just say if it's time to "go big or go home," people definitely don't want you to go any bigger.*

- *You now think that a "Breakfast of Champions" is only a Sausage McMuffin on the way to practice.*

- *You married him for the sperm donation; you've kept him around for the hockey instruction.*

You know this sounds crazy, but sometimes you actually feel like you're capable of being in 2 places at 1 time.

You Might Be a ~~Crazy~~ Dedicated Hockey Mom If . . .

- *You feel most "connected" to all hockey moms (and to the universe in general) when your team is up 10-0.*

- *Your player missed school because he was sick, but he played hockey that same night.*

- *You've chewed out your husband after a men's pick-up game for "not playing up to his potential" and "setting a bad example for the children."*

It's taken you awhile, but you finally feel like you have a handle on how the whole "hockey thing" works.

You Might Be a ~~Crazy~~ Dedicated Hockey Mom If . . .

- *You sometimes worry that you "didn't get them on skates early enough."*

- *The kids break a window with a puck, and all you can think to say is "nice shot."*

- *You've added a fake-and-deke element to your Kama Sutra "moves" to keep your husband's interest during hockey season.*

You're now required to give a urine sample
before entering the local rink.

You Might Be a ~~Crazy~~ Dedicated Hockey Mom If . . .

- *You can totally relate to the Indian goddess Kali — I mean, who wouldn't want multiple arms to help them lug hockey gear, while pushing a baby carriage and carrying a tray of Timmies?*

- *There's still a swing hanging from the bedroom ceiling — that's true! — but now it's used for dryland training.*

- *You kind of hoped your husband would have an affair at some point, just so there would be someone else to help with all the driving.*

You've been the subject of a recent CBC documentary on "The Protective Instincts of Hockey Moms."

You Might Be a ~~Crazy~~ Dedicated Hockey Mom If . . .

- *You've got your book club reading Bob McKenzie's "Hockey Dad: True Confessions of a (Crazy?) Hockey Parent."*

- *After last year's playoffs, the Pastor started using you as an example of "the perils of eye-for-an-eye justice."*

- *You've had your nails done in team colours.*

Sometimes you take it upon yourself to clean the team's locker room.

You Might Be a ~~Crazy~~ Dedicated Hockey Mom If . . .

- *You think penalties should be reserved exclusively for "those dirty kids on the other team."*

- *Folks sitting directly behind you in the stands aren't sure whether to focus on your skull tattoo or your black thong.*

- *You begin every conversation with "In AAA . . ."*

There's nothing — and I mean NOTHING —you
wouldn't do to help and protect that kid of yours.

You Might Be a ~~Crazy~~ Dedicated Hockey Mom If . . .

- *You get upset when the dirty laundry "isn't sweaty enough."*

- *You credit most of the team's success to Red Bull.*

- *You might knit during the games, but let's just say that people are more than a little concerned about maintaining a safe distance from those needles.*

You use sign language to communicate from the stands.

You Might Be a ~~Crazy~~ Dedicated Hockey Mom If . . .

- *You see your main role, next to that of chauffeur, as being PR rep and agent (and if your kid doesn't have a deal done by Peewee, you'll be bitterly disappointed).*

- *You've hired a sport's psychologist to deal with your player's scoring slump.*

- *You've stopped "bothering" the kids about their homework — there's no time anyway.*

You've customized your $800 Prada handbag to carry
absolutely everything your player needs.

You Might Be a ~~Crazy~~ Dedicated Hockey Mom If . . .

- *The other parents are calling you the "cancer on the team," which makes things kind of uncomfortable — mainly because there's already someone on the team who actually does have cancer.*

- *You plan Saturday night dinners around Hockey Night in Canada.*

- *Your kids disciplinary "time-outs" at home have always been 2 minutes in duration.*

You get kind of annoyed when
the Zamboni driver "misses a spot."

You Might Be a ~~Crazy~~ Dedicated Hockey Mom If . . .

- *You've started to consider cross-border shopping only as "a good opportunity to pick up new hockey equipment."*

- *You've seen the team website, you've seen the official game sheet, and now you're asking for your player's "missing points" to be investigated.*

- *You've actually kicked a soccer mom's ass.*

You've had to go to "Plan B" to make sure your player gets treated fairly.

You Might Be a ~~Crazy~~ Dedicated Hockey Mom If . . .

- *You joined a hockey pool and picked all your players based on 2 important qualifications: hair styles and funny names.*

- *Sometimes you like to sit in the middle of the opposing team's fans — just to "live on the edge."*

- *You wear your heart on your sleeve, and no one can fault you for that . . . but that time you threw the garbage can on the ice and went after the ref — that they can fault you for.*

You are openly referred to as
"the reason he will never make the team."

2nd Period Intermission

COOKING
LESSONS

THE BEST OF
HOCKEY MOM RECIPES*

Author's note: These were the best recipes we could pull together in such short notice. Some of them don't even look that good, honestly, and I'm not intending to make them for my family — enjoy!

Short-Shift Meat Pie

A Recipe Inspired by Coach Whitman (Fergus, ON)

Ingredients:

2 pounds ground pork
1/4 teaspoon ground cloves
1/4 teaspoon nutmeg
1/2 cup chopped onion
3/4 teaspoon salt
1/2 chopped celery stalk
1 1/2 cups water
2 potatoes (mashed and pre-cooked
on your own time)
1 15 ounce refrigerated pie crust

Directions:

1. *Invite Coach over to dinner.*
2. *Mix all the ingredients together — except the pie crust! — and don't lose sight of your wine: a common rookie mistake.*
3. *Before Coach arrives, give the mixed ingredients the Charlie Simmer* treatment for approximately 3 hours.*
4. *Ding dong: Coach is here. Make sure his wine glass is always full — you want him to be 100% at ease.*
5. *Somehow put all the ingredients into the pie crust, and bake until the crust is brown. It will take about 45 minutes — at least, that's what you tell Coach.*
6. *At about the 15-second mark (coincidentally, the average length of your son's shifts), you rush over to the oven, pull out the meat pie, and serve it to (or force it on) Coach. Then, acting a little nonplussed over Coach's comments that it's not done, you say: "Of course, it's not done! It was only a 15-second shift — how could it possibly do anything in that short of time!"*
7. *You put the whole mess back in the oven, slamming the oven door loudly, as though it were a bench gate at the rink.*
8. *With arms crossed, you glance over at him every now and again, and shake your head, as though thoroughly disappointed in his attitude.*
9. *Every minute, for the next 44 3/4 minutes, you will need to check on the meat pie, announcing each time, "That's a proper one-minute shift, Coach!"**

---

*   Charlie Simmer: former L.A. King; handsome devil.

Twice-Benched Potatoes

Yet Another Recipe Inspired by Coach Whitman (Fergus, ON)

Ingredients:

17 large potatoes
That's it

Directions:

1. *Invite Coach over for dinner again. He might be somewhat reluctant — understandably so — after the "meat pie ambush." If you need to apologize, do so. Tell him you have a new recipe that you simply must share with him (and the meal will be fully cooked this time), as a way of making amends.*
2. *Bake 17 potatoes at whatever temperature you like.*
3. *"Here comes Coach now — give him a beer this time; let him put his feet up; ask him about his coaching philosophy; get him talking, opening up.*
4. *Bzzz. Bzzz. The egg timer rings just in time.*
5. *You take the potatoes out of the oven — did I mention that you should have carved them all to look like players' helmets?*
6. *Add sour cream (low fat?), butter, chives, and bacon bits to the table.*
7. *Encourage Coach to play with his food, using all 17 potatoes. Tell him you know it's not always easy, but, you add, "Just watch me do it first."*
8. *Juggle them 3 at a time; 5 at a time; show him: it's like poetry in motion.*
9. *Talk to them: "What's that, Jake? You got baked on that last play. Ha ha ha."*
10. *Now move them all over to coach — except one; you put that one aside.*
11. *Now encourage Coach to play with ALL his potatoes. When he reaches for the lone potato, strike his hand immediately (preferably with a stick). "You can't play with that one any more," you say. "You benched him, remember? And now my little potato doesn't want to play any more — his confidence, mashed."*

My Little Goal-Scorer Angel Cake

A Recipe Shared by Martha Winsbury (Windsor, NS)

Ingredients:

<u>Batch 1</u>
1 cup sifted cake flour
1 teaspoon salt
1 cup sugar

<u>Batch 2</u>
12 large egg whites
2 tablespoons water
1 teaspoon vanilla extract
1 teaspoon almond extract
1 teaspoon cream of tartar
1 tablespoon lemon juice
50 loonies

Directions:

1. Beat batch 1 in a large bowl until tired or foamy.
2. Add batch 2 slowly, beating it repeatedly until back goes out or stiff.
3. Bake at 350° C for 45 minutes.
4. Serve with a sugar glaze in your team's colours.
5. Write on the cake (with icing) how many goals your player has scored so far (padding numbers is acceptable).
6. Bring the cake to the rink and turn it into a big production. Gather the whole team — parents and kids — together. Just before game time is usually recommended.
7. "No, it's no one's birthday," you answer the kids. "I just thought it's important that we take a moment to celebrate (and thank) my Bobby for all the goals he has scored for us this season."
8. Then, talking very slowly, you explain to them gently that Bobby's place is at the top of the cake, because he is the best player; whereas their place is on the bottom, which is a little like their place on the bench.
9. Have all the players count out Bobby's goals. Alternatively, they can shout them out: "Do you have 1? Do you have 2?" And so on.
10. Finally, encourage the kids to look for the "hidden loonies" in the cake, explaining to them that they should consider these as "pre-payment" for future assists on Bobby's goals.

Omelette in a Bag

A Recipe Shared by Jean Winslop (Calgary, AB)

Ingredients:

Bag
8 eggs
Shake of Allspice
Leftovers, maybe some meat?
Red peppers and sun-dried tomatoes

Directions:

1. *You simply wake up late for practice, and stagger — half-awake — towards the fridge with plastic bag in hand.*
2. *Crack and dump the egg ingredients into bag.*
3. *Tie bag, and head for minivan (with player).*
4. *On the way to the rink, crank your heater to about 400° C and tie bag to heater.*
5. *After 5 minutes, remove bag, shake, and re-attach to heater.*
6. *Wait (and keep driving).*
7. *After 15 minutes, detach bag (before it explodes).*
8. *Serve (or pour) with whatever drinks or food stuffs are lying around on floor in minivan.*
9. *In retrospect, this is really more of a "guy recipe" . . .*

Chicken S*#t Sandwiches

A Recipe Shared by Coach Whitman (Fergus, ON)

Ingredients:

Whole chicken (pre-grilled is best, as post-game grilling can be brutal)
Loaf of bread (they say the whole wheat stuff is better for you)
1 cup butter

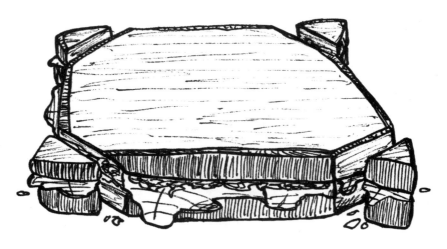

Directions:

I used to eat out all the time (the joys of bachelorhood!), and wasn't really interested in cooking, until this one crazy hockey mom started inviting me over to her place to try these new recipes she'd concocted. That's when I started cooking for the team.

1. *It's really easy — just stick the chicken in the bread to make sandwiches.*
2. *Cut the corners off each sandwich.*
3. *Bring the sandwiches to the rink and leave them out after the game.*
4. *When the players ask how they played, tell them, "You did OK."*
5. *Show them the tray of sandwiches and ask, "Who's hungry?"*
6. *"Say, wait a second — there's something missing from the sandwiches. Who knows what's missing?" you ask, in the voice of a trained professional.*
7. *Your brightest player will then put up his hand and proudly announce: "The corners are missing."*
8. *"Exactly!" you reply. "We know how much you all hate going into the corners, so we cut them off for you. Do you want us to chew the food for you as well?"*

Editor's note: After submitting this recipe, Coach Whitman — and we heard this second hand — was actually torn apart and eaten (yes, eaten) by the team's parents. We tell you this, dear reader, as a cautionary note, so you are fully aware of any and all inherent risks involved in trying the Chicken S*#t Sandwich recipe.

2 Cows in the Garage

A Recipe Shared by Emily Drylander (Winnipeg, MB)

Ingredients:

2 frozen cows (whole)

2 over-sized meat hooks

1 cold garage

94

Directions:

This recipe requires some advance explanation. We all know the importance of dryland training for building the strength, speed and agility required to play competitive sports. We also understand the importance of a high protein diet. I have combined the 2 ideas in my "2 Cows in the Garage Diet and Training Regimen."

1. *Simply hang 2 frozen cows from the rafters in your garage, and encourage your player — puck on stick; stick in hand — to "split the D."*
2. *Then, with your player standing "at the ready" in his "hockey stance" between the 2 cows, pull and swing each cow towards him.*
3. *"Bend at the knees! Lean into the cow!" — this is always good instruction.*
4. *Repeat these drills until you're satisfied that he's actually beating the cows to the puck.*
5. *Then, move one of the cows to the corner of the garage, and instruct your player to "forecheck the cow!" The cow should be pinned firmly against the boards.*
6. *If any pieces of frozen beef become dislodged in the process, these can be your player's next pre-game meal. As we've told our boys for years — "Check what you eat."*

Easy 3-Way Meatballs

A Recipe Shared by Florence Gripper (Burnaby, BC)

Ingredients:

4 pounds ground beef
4 garlic cloves, chopped
1 cup sun-dried tomatoes
2 cups bread crumbs
2 cups parsley, chopped
2 cups grated Parmesan
2 large onions, chopped
5 teaspoons Allspice
2 cups flour
8 tablespoons olive oil
Excessive alcohol
17 toothpicks

Directions:

1. *Invite the team's parents over.*
2. *Mix all the ingredients together, lovingly shaping and forming 17 pairs of 2-inch meatballs.*
3. *Roll them around, playfully, in the flour.*
4. *Add oil to the frying pan, and then toss the meatballs in.*
5. *Fry for 10-12 minutes.*
6. *After removing the meatballs from the pan, create dumbell-like pairs using toothpicks.*
7. *After a few drinks, invite all the hockey moms into the kitchen.*
8. *Have each hockey mom choose a set of meatballs, and write her husband's name on them (somehow).*
9. *Put all the meatballs in a bowl in the center of the living room, and, at the end of the evening, each hockey mom chooses a new set of meatballs to take home.*
10. *The whole recipe gets a little fuzzy after that — improvisation may be necessary.*

Coaching Staff Waffles

A Recipe Shared by Shelby Kellogoski (Regina, SK)

Ingredients:

2 cups flour

Some baking powder (you decide?)

A sprinkle (or dash?) of sugar

A handful of butter

Some eggs

Milk (from a cow)

Salt

Strawberries

Whipped cream

A lot of indecision

Directions:

We used to call our coaching staff "Snap, Crackle, and Pop," but lately they've become a different breakfast food entirely. Their indecisiveness of late was the inspiration behind the Coaching Staff Waffles recipe.

1. *Start whenever you're ready . . .*
2. *Just tell us "when" . . .*
3. *Blend the dry stuff, and whisk the wet stuff.*
4. *We should probably take a vote on what to do next, unless you just want to use the waffle iron?*
5. *Add strawberries and whipped cream.*
6. *Present (or don't present) to coaching staff.*
7. *In fact, it's not a bad idea to throw these on the ice whenever you think a "waffle call" has been made. It shows you're paying attention, and allows you to be removed from a game you can sometimes no longer bear to watch.*

Treasure-Hunt Pemmican

A Recipe Shared by "Digger" (Flin Flon, MB)

Ingredients:

Any kind of dried meat
(can be deer, moose, elk —
whatever is easiest to kill with your bow and arrow)
Meat rack
Plastic bags
Shovel (or augur)

Directions:

This recipe is for the cost-conscious hockey mom, who can't stand to pay rink-concession prices (for foods that are unhealthy anyway).

1. *Early in the summer, well before hockey season, review the list of teams in your loop for the upcoming season.*
2. *Map out the arena locations.*
3. *Take a week off work.*
4. *Send your husband on a hunting expedition with one simple instruction: "Kill something and bring it home."*
5. *Start a fire on your lawn, and hang the carcass on a meat rack nearby.*
6. *Let it dry in the sun (and fire) for one full day.*
7. *Chop the meat into chunks and pulverize it.*
8. *Put out fire.*
9. *Drive to the first arena on your list, and, finding a grassy area behind it, dig a 1' x 1' hole and bury the dried meat in a plastic bag.*
10. *Repeat at each arena location.*
11. *Avoid police.*
12. *When hockey season starts, simply locate and dig up your newly-made pemmican, and there you have it — a pre-game meal for the whole family.*

You Might Be a ~~Crazy~~ Dedicated Hockey Mom If . . .

- *You've started working on your upper body strength, just so you can tie his skates tighter.*

- *You're considered a bit of a jello-shooter "artiste" at team parties.*

- *You've made permanent hand marks on the arena glass.*

You're personally responsible for the new acronym "HMILF."

You Might Be a ~~Crazy~~ Dedicated Hockey Mom If . . .

- *You're seriously considering a "boob job" just to help you stay warm at the rink.*

- *You think your team fees should be reduced, because your kid is "obviously better than the rest of them."*

- *You're using a greasier shampoo, hoping it will help you slip more easily out of post-game headlocks.*

You've started to consider a 2-hour drive to games or practices a "reasonable amount of time."

You Might Be a ~~Crazy~~ Dedicated Hockey Mom If . . .

- *You're known (and have actually received orders) for your hash brownies at parties.*

- *You tell everyone that your player's "soft hands" come from your side of the family.*

- *The coach made a 3-way trade that somehow involved you but not your player.*

You give your player the VIP treatment on game days,
because you don't want him to be distracted by the
"less-skilled members of his family."

You Might Be a ~~Crazy~~ Dedicated Hockey Mom If . . .

- *You've sent out drunken emails questioning the coach on the value of "hard work" and "team play" — but, then again, . . . who hasn't?*

- *"Coach shopping" now means buying a present for the bench boss.*

- *Some people say you have twins — but you refer to them as "coincidental minors."*

You actually enjoy fundraising events.

You Might Be a Crazy Dedicated Hockey Mom If . . .

- *The assistant coach's main job is to "contain you."*

- *You're on the Rink Poutine Diet — and it's just not working.*

- *You see arena conversations as opportunities to talk about your kid's play . . . followed by, quite honestly, some blah-blah-blah boring stuff that's not worth listening to about other people's kids.*

You've dressed up as a "puck bunny" on Halloween,
just to get your husband's attention.

You Might Be a ~~Crazy~~ Dedicated Hockey Mom If . . .

- *When you watch the games, the main thing you're looking for is the answer to the question: "Did they sleep and eat enough?"*

- *Family dinners are typically served with everyone sitting down together . . . in the minivan on the way to a game.*

- *You shout out questions during the game, and then shout out answers in another voice.*

You're the only one who seems to have
"assigned seating" in the stands.

You Might Be a ~~Crazy~~ Dedicated Hockey Mom If . . .

- *Your sales in team fundraising are actually higher than your sales at work.*

- *You've criticized players for "not taking enough penalties."*

- *E-Harmony lists "must love hockey" as your #1 requirement in a mate.*

The Best Get-Out-of-Work-Early-for-Hockey Excuses

1. *Someone died (no "double-burying," please!)*
2. *Customer visits or "store checks" (conveniently, near rink)*
3. *Flu symptoms (insert drama)*
4. *Working from home (yeah, you and Ferris Bueller . . .)*
5. *"Female emergency" (works with male boss only)*
6. *Say you have to "get something from the car," and then just drive off . . .*
7. *"Staying home sick" (of work) — sometimes it's easier just to stay home — clock-watching can be agonizing!*
8. *Out buying a gift for a co-worker or boss (how thoughtful!)*
9. *Doctor/dentist appointment (remember: you're in pain)*
10. *Jury duty (save this one for weekday tournaments)*

You Might Be a Crazy Dedicated Goalie Mom If . . .

- *You're starting to think the G-Spot is only the goalie position.*

- *There are 2 goalies on the team, but it's still not clear to you why your kid doesn't play each and every game.*

- *They see new pads; you see personal bankruptcy.*

You're having recurring nightmares
about your goalie's "5-hole problem."

You Might Be a ~~Crazy~~ Dedicated Goalie Mom If . . .

- *You're prone to stretching the truth a little when it comes to recording the shots against.*

- *Well, it's not that you wish your team's other goalie will play poorly; it's just, well, . . . you wish that your own kid will play that much better.*

- *You're paranoid that everyone is gossiping about your kid after every loss (and you would be right).*

You're a founding member of a Goalie Support Group.

Post-Game Analysis

Take the Crazy
(Or Just Very Dedicated?)
Hockey Mom Test*

* And you can always just ignore the results.

1. *The coach's 24-hour rule is:*

      a) a good idea, as it allows for "cooler heads to prevail"

      b) a rule to be followed and respected

      c) a chance to rethink what I was going to tell him

      d) a suggestion that applies only to other people

2. *My behaviour in the stands is:*

      a) a reflection of my general persona at home and in the workplace

      b) a glowing example to all the other parents

      c) always positive and beyond reproach

      d) something I can remember only under deep hypnosis

3. *The majority of my hockey-mom dealings with the police have been:*

      a) connected to my extensive volunteer work with various charities

      b) confined to calling Tipsters for extra cash

      c) limited to the odd speeding violation

      d) surprise appearances next to me at the arena

4. The first thing I think of when I look at the ink blot below is . . .

    a) a lot of ink
    b) the male sex organ
    c) those miniature sausages that sometimes go on sale at the
       deli
    d) someone is trying to hurt "my baby"

5. *The other teams' hockey moms are:*

>   *a) women with whom I have a lot in common*
>   *b) funny, engaging moms who love their kids as much as I*
>   *love mine*
>   *c) to be admired for all the "running around" they do*
>   *d) delusional*

6. *Proper hockey rink attire includes:*

>   *a) dressing warmly and appropriately for a public setting*
>   *b) remembering not to wear flip-flops as the weather turns*
>   *colder*
>   *c) bringing the community blanket to share with friends*
>   *d) clothes I wouldn't let my teenage daughter wear*

7. *The best way to avoid arena conflicts is to:*

>   *a) walk away*
>   *b) return abuse with kind words*
>   *c) be the bigger person and bite your tongue*
>   *d) end it quickly and decisively*

8. *My feelings towards referees are:*

  a) similar to my feelings about pesticides — I know they're necessary, but I try to avoid thinking about them

  b) ambivalent at best

  c) clouded by my general resentment of authority figures

  d) 100% determined by whether or not we are winning

9. *I have emailed the Convenor with a complaint:*

  a) never

  b) once in a while

  c) only when there was a serious problem

  d) just now

10. *The best way to describe my child's place on the team is:*

  a) a very social person

  b) a good listener who will follow the coach's lead

  c) a hard worker who is learning and having fun

  d) a gift that is not fully appreciated

11. *The last thing I remember about the team party was:*

      a) the food being brought out

      b) the "shooter girl" hovering in the vicinity of my table

      c) dancing on the table

      d) buying the tickets

12. *The main thing I look for in a mate is:*

      a) financial well being

      b) love and respect

      c) sexual attractiveness

      d) the ability to drive my kid to games

13. *The odds of my player making the NHL are:*

      a) about the same as the odds of winning the lottery

      b) lower than the odds of getting hit by lightning

      c) marginal at best, but I never want to kill his dreams

      d) pretty good, actually — thanks for asking

Test Results

Incorrect Answer Keys:

1. *d*
2. *d*
3. *d . . . seems like a lot of 'd's*
4. *Answers will vary.*
5. *They all sound good.*
6. *d*
7. *d*
8. *d*
9. *d*
10. *d*
11. *d*
12. *They're all very reasonable.*
13. *d*

If you answered with mostly a's, b's, or c's (and only the odd "d"), then CONGRATULATIONS, you're not completely crazy — just crazy about your kid.